mrjc
7/13

WASHINGTON'S CROSSING

THE

DELAWARE

AND THE

WINTER AT VALLEY FORGE—

THROUGH

PRIMARY SOURCES

John Micklos, Jr.

Enslow Publishers, Inc.
40 Industrial Road
Box 398
Berkeley Heights, NJ 07922
USA

http://www.enslow.com

Original edition published as *Crossing the Delaware and Valley Forge: Two Wild Winters With Washington* in 2008.

Library of Congress Cataloging-in-Publication Data

Micklos, John.
  Washington's crossing the Delaware and the winter at Valley Forge : through primary sources / John Micklos, Jr.
      p. cm. — (The American Revolution through primary sources)
  "Original edition published as Crossing the Delaware and Valley Forge: Two Wild Winters With Washington in 2008."
  Includes bibliographical references and index.
  Summary: "Explores two pivotal winters with George Washington's army during the American Revolution, including his crossing of the Delaware River, the battles at Trenton and Princeton, and the winter at Valley Forge"—Provided by publisher.
  ISBN 978-0-7660-4132-5
  1. Washington, George, 1732–1799—Headquarters—Pennsylvania—Valley Forge—Juvenile literature. 2. Washington, George, 1732–1799—Headquarters—New Jersey. 3. United States. Continental Army—Military life—Juvenile literature. 4. Valley Forge (Pa.)—History, Military—18th century—Juvenile literature. 5. New Jersey—History—Revolution, 1775-1783—Campaigns—Juvenile literature. 6. Pennsylvania—History—Revolution, 1775–1783—Campaigns—Juvenile literature. 7. United States—History—Revolution, 1775–1783—Campaigns—Juvenile literature. I. Title.
  E234.M53 2013
  973.3'341—dc23

          2012022416

Future editions:
Paperback ISBN 978-1-4644-0190-9
ePUB ISBN 978-1-4645-1103-5
PDF ISBN 978-1-4646-1103-2

Printed in the United States of America

082012 Lake Book Manufacturing, Inc., Melrose Park, IL

10 9 8 7 6 5 4 3 2 1

To Our Readers: We have done our best to make sure all Internet Addresses in this book were active and appropriate when we went to press. However, the author and the publisher have no control over and assume no liability for the material available on those Internet sites or on other Web sites they may link to. Any comments or suggestions can be sent by email to comments@enslow.com or to the address on the back cover.

♻ Enslow Publishers, Inc., is committed to printing our books on recycled paper. The paper in every book contains 10% to 30% post-consumer waste (PCW). The cover board on the outside of each book contains 100% PCW. Our goal is to do our part to help young people and the environment too!

Illustration Credits: © Brianna May / Photos.com, p. 18; Domenick D'Andrea, courtesy of the National Guard, p. 9; Genvessel, p. 4; The Granger Collection, NYC, p. 28; The John F. Reed Collection, Valley Forge National Historical Park, p. 29; Library of Congress Geography and Map Division, p. 41; Library of Congress Manuscript Division, p. 6; Library of Congress Prints and Photographs, pp. 1, 3, 5, 15, 20, 21, 23, 31, 37, 40; Shutterstock.com, p. 25; Superstock / Everett Collection, pp. 12–13; Courtesy of the U.S. Navy Art Collection, Washington, D.C., p. 35; Valley Forge National Historic Park, pp. 32, 33.

Cover Illustration: Library of Congress Prints and Photographs (George Washington crossing the Delaware River).

CONTENTS

LOOK FOR THIS SYMBOL **Primary Source** TO FIND THE PRIMARY SOURCES THROUGHOUT THIS BOOK.

A view of the Delaware River from Trenton, New Jersey during winter. General George Washington had to contend with a dangerous winter storm and the icy conditions similar to those seen in this photograph.

CHAPTER 1

★

DESPERATE TIMES

The wind howled. Rain and sleet pelted the soldiers as they made their way across the Delaware River on a fleet of small boats. Still, General George Washington was determined to cross the river on Christmas night, 1776. He planned to attack an outpost of the British army in Trenton, New Jersey.

Most armies did not fight during the winter. Bad weather and bad roads made it too difficult to move troops. Therefore, this winter attack might surprise the enemy. Washington knew his plan was risky. If the attack failed, his army might be trapped in New Jersey. The larger British army could crush his small force. That might spell the end of the American fight for freedom.

PRIMARY SOURCE

In July 1775, the Continental Congress issued this document commissioning George Washington as commander-in-chief of the Continental Army.

Still, Washington knew he had to take the chance. His army was close to falling apart. Morale was low. Many of his troops were due to go home at the end of the year. Few planned to reenlist, or rejoin the army, at that time. Washington feared there might soon be no army at all unless he did something to rally the troops' spirits.

How had the army come to this point? Emotions ran high following the American Revolution's opening battles at Lexington and Concord, Massachusetts, in April 1775. Then, in June, the British attacked Americans dug in at Breed's Hill and Bunker Hill, north of Boston. British commanders expected an easy victory there. But the Americans fought bravely, and the British suffered heavy casualties in the battle. More than a thousand redcoats (British soldiers) were killed or wounded before the Americans finally retreated.

Soon after, Washington was named commander-in-chief of the newly formed Continental Army. Months passed. The British army remained trapped inside Boston. Finally, in March 1776, they abandoned the city. They boarded ships and sailed away.

On July 4, Congress approved the Declaration of Independence. It stated clearly why the Americans were fighting. Morale among the Continental Army was high.

Then, throughout the summer of 1776, things began to go wrong. Washington had positioned his soldiers to protect New

York City from British attack. The British had more troops. They had more cannons. They had ships to move their troops quickly. Twice, on Long Island and at White Plains, the British defeated Washington's troops in battle. Both times, Washington's army barely escaped being destroyed.

Escape in the Night

After the defeat on Long Island, Washington's army was nearly trapped by the British. On the night of August 29, his troops began to slip across the East River to Manhattan a few at a time on boats. They moved quietly. If the British realized what was happening, they could attack. Then the whole army might be destroyed. As dawn came, a dense fog fell. This helped cover the troop movement. In all, some 9,000 soldiers moved to safety overnight. The army survived to fight again.[1]

Continental Army soldiers exchange musket fire with British redcoats during the Battle of Long Island. The British soundly defeated Washington's army in this battle.

By late October, the British controlled New York City. Then, on November 16, they captured Fort Washington just outside of New York. More than 2,800 American troops were killed, wounded, or captured. Washington blamed himself for the defeat.[2]

As a result of these losses, Washington formed a new strategy for the war. He went on the defensive. He would not "put anything to the [risk]" in a major battle unless he had no other choice.[3]

Still, he needed to fight enough so that his troops and the Continental Congress did not get too discouraged. "On every side there is a choice of difficulties," he wrote.[4]

Washington's troops retreated across New Jersey. The British army followed close behind, but did not launch a full attack. General William Howe, the British commander, wanted to set up outposts throughout New Jersey. As in most areas, many people in New Jersey were still loyal to the king. Howe hoped to convince others to abandon the rebellion. Besides, cold weather was coming. Howe wanted to get his troops into their winter quarters. He did not want to fight again until spring.

Other British generals disagreed. Some wanted to pursue and destroy Washington's army. Others wanted to capture Philadelphia and arrest members of the Continental Congress. They thought this might end the rebellion. Eventually, Howe's plan of building outposts won out. This plan had one weakness, however. It gave Washington time to regroup.[5]

Famous Painting

It became one of the most famous images in history. George Washington stands near the front of a boat crossing an ice-choked river. Some soldiers propel the boat forward with poles. Others hold the American flag. Still others huddle low in the boat. All seem to have an expression of quiet determination.

The scene comes from *Washington Crossing the Delaware*, painted in 1851 by Emanuel Leutze. The painting captures the urgent mood of the desperate attack. It portrays Washington as the strong leader he was. Today, the painting hangs in New York's Metropolitan Museum of Art.[6]

While the British argued, Washington's troops moved across New Jersey. Finally, they retreated across the Delaware River from Trenton into Pennsylvania. The troops gathered every boat they could find and brought them across the river. They hoped this would keep the British from following them.[7]

Still, the situation was bleak. The enlistment period for many of Washington's troops was due to expire at the end of the year.

Many planned to go home then. Washington feared that unless some reenlisted and some new recruits joined, "the game is pretty near up."[8]

At the same time, Washington gave thought to a "counter stroke."[9] Using information from a local spy, Washington made

In 1851, Emanuel Leutze completed this famous painting of George Washington and his soldiers crossing the Delaware River on December 25, 1776. The dramatic painting portrays the great leadership and determination of Washington, however, it does not give an accurate representation of the actual river crossing.

plans to attack Trenton. This British outpost was manned by a force of Hessian soldiers. Hessians were Germans who had been hired by the British to fight on their side during the war.

At 4:00 P.M. on Christmas, American drums began to beat. The troops lined up. They knew something special was happening.

According to sixteen-year-old soldier John Greenwood, he and the other troops carried their muskets, many rounds of ammunition, and three days of cooked rations. They sensed a battle was coming.[10]

They were right. Using the boats the army had gathered, Washington planned to move his troops across the river during the night. They would cross at three different points. About 1,500 men were to cross the river at Bristol. To create confusion, these men would attack the enemy south of Trenton. A 700-man force would land right near Trenton. This group would set up positions to block a Hessian retreat. The main force, about 2,400 men, would cross the Delaware nine miles north of Trenton. After marching south, this force would launch a surprise attack on Trenton just before dawn.

The plan seemed simple. Making it work turned out to be much harder. The troop movements had to run on schedule. And the weather that night almost spoiled everything.

CHAPTER 2

★

ATTACK IN THE SNOW

From the beginning, the attack ran behind schedule. Many troops were ill. Others did not have proper clothing. One American officer, Major James Wilkinson, later wrote that here and there the snow was red "with blood from the feet of the men who wore broken shoes."[1]

Still, the men pressed forward. They knew how vital the mission was. The password was "victory or death."[2]

Soon, the weather turned bad. When the troops started out, the sun was shining bright. By the time they reached the river, heavy rain pelted down. Later that evening, the winter storm grew even worse. John Greenwood later recalled that "it rained, hailed, snowed, and froze."[3]

All this made the task of crossing the river harder. Even worse, great chunks of ice floated in the river. Of Washington's three forces, two were unable to get across the river. The one that did— the main force commanded by Washington—used freight boats, ferries, and any other boats they could find. Skilled watermen helped guide the boats against the swift currents and through the thick ice.[4]

Once across the river, Washington worried about what to do next. The attack was three hours behind schedule. There was no hope of reaching Trenton before daybreak. Now the Hessians might see them coming and prepare for the attack.

Washington thought about calling off the mission. But he also knew that quitting would further damage the morale of his army and the entire country. In the end, he "determined to push on at all events."[5]

Party Myth

Some accounts of the Battle of Trenton have claimed that the Hessian soldiers were slow to react to Washington's attack because they were still drunk from their Christmas celebrations. Today, many scholars dispute that claim. The Hessians had been on guard against American raids for some time. They did not expect to be attacked during such bad weather, however. That, along with the size of the attack, caught them by surprise.[6]

As daybreak neared, the army slogged on through the snow to Trenton. The men were exhausted from the effort of crossing the river. Washington rode alongside the soldiers. He encouraged them to keep going. "Advance and charge," he urged them.[7]

The army reached Trenton a little after 8 A.M. Daylight had broken, but the snow made it hard to see. Near the edge of town, a Hessian soldier emerged from a guardhouse. Soon, other Hessians and the Americans exchanged fire.

The Americans surged forward. Colonel Johann Rall, the Hessian commander, ordered a counterattack. Fighting raged through the streets of Trenton. The Americans rained a barrage of cannon fire and musket fire on the Hessian troops. Colonel Rall fell, hit by two bullets. Soon after, the Hessians surrendered.

PRIMARY SOURCE

During the Battle of Trenton, Washington's soldiers barraged the Hessians with cannon fire in the streets of the town. The British used this colonial-era cannon to fend off American and French attacks in Yorktown, Virginia.

In all, the Hessians lost about 1,000 men killed, wounded, or captured. No American troops were killed in the battle. Only a few were wounded. It was a huge victory for Washington's army.[8]

The troops had little time to celebrate. They had to retreat back across the Delaware River before more British soldiers arrived. Washington praised his troops for their "spirited and gallant behavior."[9]

News of the battle traveled quickly. Across America, people rejoiced. British leaders were dismayed.

Washington decided to press the attack. A few days later, his weary army crossed the Delaware River again. In New Jersey, he called the troops together. Many of their enlistments ended on December 31. They would be free to go home. Washington pleaded with the soldiers to remain with the army for a few more weeks. "Your country is at stake," he said.[10] He offered an incentive, or bonus, of $10 (about $230 in today's money) to men who stayed. To his relief, many did so.

George Washington reviews the captured British flags as his soldiers take a needed rest after the American victory in the Battle of Trenton.

Soon, a large British force commanded by General Charles Cornwallis approached. The two armies skirmished at Trenton on January 2. Cornwallis had more men. If he had pressed on, he might have destroyed the smaller American army. Instead, he chose to rest his weary troops until the next day.

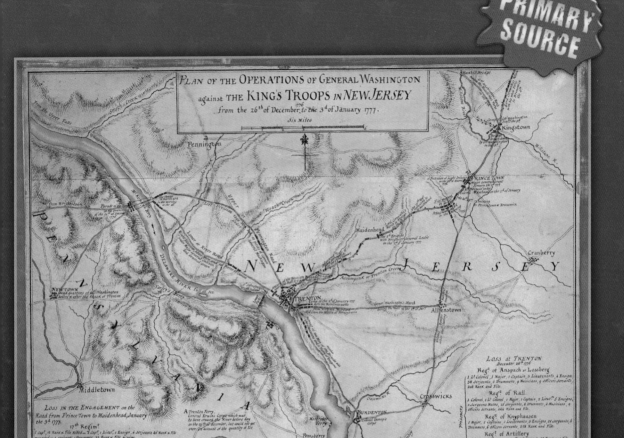

Less than a week after the victory at Trenton, Washington led his troops on a bold march to Princeton, where the Americans claimed victory again. These two important victories required great planning and military tactics. This 1777 map shows Washington's plan of operations from December 26 to January 3 in the battles of Trenton and Princeton.

"We've got the Old Fox safe now," Cornwallis said. "We'll go over and bag him in the morning."[11]

By morning, however, the fox had escaped. During the night, Washington led his troops on a bold march toward Princeton. He left behind just a few soldiers to keep the campfires burning. The British thought his army was still there.

Washington's troops fought with redcoats at Princeton. After heavy fighting, the Americans captured the town. They had only a handful of casualties. The British lost about 300 dead or wounded. Another 300 were captured.[12]

Americans cheered these victories. They now believed they could defeat the British. In two daring strokes, Washington had changed the momentum of the war.

CHAPTER 3

★

THE CAMP AT VALLEY FORGE

A year later, the Continental Army once again straggled into winter quarters in Pennsylvania. As had been the case the year before, they had suffered some key defeats. On September 11, 1777, they lost a hard-fought battle at Brandywine. About two weeks later, the British captured the American capital of Philadelphia.

Still, Washington and his army had hope. They knew they had fought well. Indeed, Congress wanted Washington to try to recapture Philadelphia. On October 4, the Americans mounted a large surprise attack at Germantown, north of the city. That attack failed, however. Washington knew his army was not strong enough to drive the British out of Philadelphia. It would be hard to conduct any campaign as winter began.

In the end, Washington decided to spend the winter at Valley Forge, Pennsylvania, about twenty miles from Philadelphia. From there, Washington could keep watch on the British army. Yet Valley Forge was far enough away that the British could not launch a surprise attack. Also, the area was well protected by hills and rivers. In many ways, the location was perfect.[1]

In other ways, spending the winter at Valley Forge posed problems. The area did not have enough food to supply an army. Even fresh water was sometimes scarce. One more factor made these problems worse. The system Congress had set up for supplying the troops did not work well. As the winter of 1777 approached, the system was in chaos.[2]

The British army was well fed and warm in Philadelphia. The Continental Army needed to get its own food and shelter. As soon as the troops arrived in Valley Forge in early December, they started building log huts. These huts would be their home for

In the winter of 1777–1778, Continental soldiers built wooden huts as their living quarters in Valley Forge. This reconstructed soldiers' hut stands at Valley Forge National Historic Park in Pennsylvania.

the winter. The building process went slowly. The troops faced a shortage of tools. Many of the men lacked shoes and warm clothing. This made it hard to work in the cold. Again, part of the problem was the poor supply system. Private Joseph Plumb Martin wrote that many men were "shirtless and barefoot."[3]

Hunger posed an even worse problem. The daily food rations the troops were supposed to get—including flour or bread; beef, fish, pork, or bacon; and whiskey or some other strong alcoholic drink—were often unavailable. Some troops lived for days at a time on firecakes. These were a mixture of flour and water, cooked on griddles over the fires of the camp. In disgust, some troops chanted, "No meat! No meat!"[4]

Over the years, much has been written about the hard winter at Valley Forge. In truth, the weather was not that harsh. It was

Home Sweet Hut

Soldiers at Valley Forge lived in wooden huts. Each hut was fourteen by sixteen feet and housed twelve men. Soldiers cut down trees and dragged the wood to the campsite. They packed clay between the wooden logs to keep the cold out. Each hut had a fireplace and chimney. The better the men built the huts, the warmer they were during the winter.

The Conway Cabal

Even as the winter at Valley Forge threatened Washington's army, politics threatened Washington himself. Some members of Congress thought he was unfit for command. Others feared he was setting himself up to become a dictator. Some wanted to replace him with General Horatio Gates.

Thomas Conway, a new brigadier general, wrote a letter to Gates calling Washington a "weak general."[5] Washington found out about this insult. Angry letters passed back and forth among Conway, Gates, and Washington. But Congress rallied around Washington. Conway soon resigned from the army. He never planned to lead a mutiny against Washington. Still, the affair became known to history as "the Conway Cabal." (A cabal is a group of secret plotters.)

not all that cold. There was not much snow. There was a lot of rain, though. Heavy rains in February made it even harder to transport supplies across bad roads.[6]

Many soldiers died of disease that winter. Without proper food and clothing, many men caught colds. Often this led

Freezing Continental soldiers warm themselves during the winter. Washington's troops suffered through a very harsh winter at Valley Forge, including bad weather, a lack of food, and poor clothing and supplies.

to pneumonia. Others grew ill because of dirty water and poor sanitation. Typhus caused many deaths. This disease is carried by lice. It is marked by fever and a rash. In one hospital during the winter of 1777–1778, an estimated 35 percent of the patients died. Most died of typhus.[7]

Other soldiers left when their enlistment time was up. Some had not been paid in months. Washington watched his army grow smaller and weaker. He pleaded with Congress for more

Head Quarters Valley Forge 5th June 1778

Sir

William Erskine Esqr who is appointed Military Surveyor and Geographer is now here, and is desiring to arrange that department — fix upon the proper number of Deputies — and settle their Pay, appointments &c. To do this, he would wish to see and consult you. I therefore desire you to come down immediately upon the receipt of this. If the movement of the Enemy from Philada. should oblige the Army to quit this ground before you arrive, I will leave directions for you. I imagine the Business you are at present upon, cannot suffer by a temporary absence.

I am Sir
Your most obt. Servt.
Go Washington

This is a letter dated June 5, 1778, written by Washington at his headquarters in Valley Forge. During the winter, Washington wrote to Congress many times to request money and supplies for his tired soldiers.

money and supplies. He worried that there might not even be an army by the time spring came.

By early February, Washington wrote that the army was in a "starving condition."[8] Soon after, Washington asked General Nathanael Greene to become the army's quartermaster general—the person in charge of supplies. Greene was one of the Continental Army's most capable officers. He soon made the supply system work better.

Around the same time, another person who would make a big difference entered the camp at Valley Forge. His name was Friedrich Wilhelm von Steuben. Von Steuben was from the German kingdom of Prussia. He had fought in wars in Europe, and he knew how to organize soldiers. He volunteered for the job of training the Continental troops to follow orders more quickly and to work together more effectively. Over the next few months, his efforts helped transform Washington's army.

CHAPTER 4

⭐

FORMING A FIGHTING FORCE

On March 19, von Steuben began working with one hundred soldiers. These men were chosen from all fourteen of the army's brigades.[1] Von Steuben's drill was simple. Back and forth the men marched. They learned how to march in step. They learned how to place themselves in battle formation. They learned how to fire and reload more quickly. They learned how to use their bayonets.

Von Steuben did not know much English. Sometimes he acted out what he wanted the soldiers to do. When the men did not do what he wanted, he cursed at them in broken English. But the soldiers respected him. They saw the value in drilling

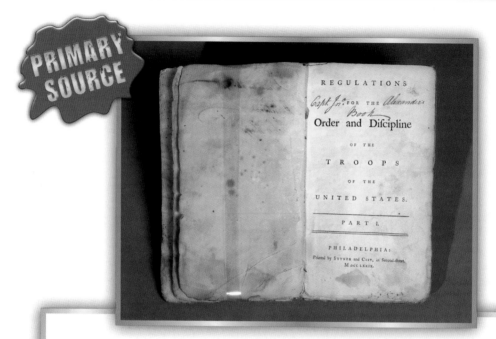

PRIMARY SOURCE

Friedrich von Steuben trained General Washington's soldiers at Valley Forge in many of the army basics, such as marching in step, loading and firing a musket, and using a bayonet. This photo shows pages from von Steuben's training manual called *Regulations for the Order and Discipline of the Troops of the United States.*

and training. They wanted to be able to match the highly-trained British troops in battle.

Soon, the entire army was using these drills. The officers observed to make sure their men did things right. Colonel Henry Knox, who returned to camp after two months in New England,

Life in Camp

Boring! That is the best word to describe life in an army camp during the winter. All soldiers who were healthy had tasks to perform each day. They might serve guard duty or help gather food or firewood. Other than that, there were long stretches with little to do.

When the weather turned bitter cold or rainy, the soldiers spent most of their free time in their huts. Sometimes they played cards or marbles. Some read. Others sang or played instruments. A few ventured out during winter to go skating on the frozen river. As the weather grew warmer, some men played games outdoors.

PRIMARY SOURCE

Life at the winter camp was often boring for the soldiers. Music was one way the men amused themselves. This jaw harp, a musical instrument, was used at Valley Forge.

noticed a big change. He wrote that the army was "improving in discipline and increasing in numbers every day."[2]

As spring came, the news grew better for the army on all fronts. The soldiers no longer suffered from the cold weather. Supplies of food and clothing improved. The army's ranks swelled as new recruits joined. The soldiers believed they were becoming a better fighting force. They felt ready to take on the British.

Then, in early May, came news that boosted spirits even higher. General Washington announced that a formal alliance with France had been formed. This was good news indeed. France had a strong army. It had a navy that could compete with the British at sea. It had lots of money that could be used to support the American cause. To celebrate, the American troops at Valley Forge marched in a grand review.

France's involvement in the war forced the British to move some of their ships and troops away from the war in America. They feared the French might strike at English-held islands in the West Indies. They even worried that France might attack

France's involvement in the war greatly aided the American cause. The French navy was powerful and could compete with Great Britain's. In this illustration, the French and British navies exchange fire during the Battle of the Virginia Capes on September 5, 1781.

A Peace Proposal

In April 1778, England offered a peace proposal. Under its terms, the British would give up the right to tax the colonies. They would renew trade with America. They would grant pardons for those who had fought against England. They would not, however, grant independence.

Congress turned down the offer. Congress said England first needed to withdraw its army and navy. Then it would have to recognize American independence. Only then could there be peace. The British did not accept those terms. The war continued.

England itself. All of these concerns kept the British from focusing completely on America.

As summer neared, Washington's troops grew eager for battle. They wanted to try out the things they had learned. Soon, they would get their chance.

CHAPTER 5

⭐

OUT INTO THE FIELD

In the spring of 1778, the British decided to leave Philadelphia. They planned to station their army, which was now under the command of Sir Henry Clinton, in New York City. In mid-June, both the British and American armies crossed into New Jersey.

On June 24, Washington met with his generals. Some thought they should let the British retreat without fighting them. Others wanted to start a major battle. Washington chose a middle course. His army followed the British troops, getting closer and closer. He planned to wait for a good chance to attack.

Uneasy Alliance

Many people thought the alliance with France would bring a quick end to the war. That was not the case, however. Fighting raged for three more years. It took some time for the Americans and the French to learn how to work together. Also, many in Congress did not fully trust France. Some described it as a "vulture" aiming to take advantage of America.[1]

By June 26, the British had arrived at Monmouth Court House in New Jersey. Washington's troops were nearby. Both armies rested on June 27, tired after long marches in steamy weather.

On June 28, Washington ordered General Charles Lee to attack the rear guard of the British army. When the redcoats counter-attacked, a panicked Lee ordered a retreat. Washington rode forward to find out what was happening. "What is the meaning of this?" he demanded.[2] Lee had no good answer.

General Washington stopped the retreat. Then he helped the American troops set up a defensive position. His calmness rallied the Continental soldiers.

The battle raged all afternoon in the intense heat. Many soldiers passed out from heatstroke. The British launched a series of attacks on the American line. Each time, they had to retreat. Both armies camped on the battlefield that night. Washington hoped to continue the battle in the morning. However, Clinton's army left before dawn and continued on toward New York.

The battle at Monmouth Court House was basically a draw. Yet it helped raise the morale of the Continental Army—and of the entire country in general. The Americans had fought the mighty British army evenly on an open battlefield. In the end, it was the redcoats who withdrew.

Monmouth marked the last major battle in the north. Over the next few years, more of the fighting shifted to the south. Finally, in October 1781, Washington defeated a large British force under General Cornwallis at Yorktown, Virginia. It was the last major battle of the war.

The triumph at Yorktown would never have been possible if the Continental Army had not survived the difficult winters

The Myth of Molly Pitcher

Over time, a myth arose about the battle at Monmouth Court House. The story described a young woman who carried water in a pitcher to the hot and tired soldiers. (That is how she earned the name Molly Pitcher.) There was no such woman. The name Molly Pitcher referred to many women who helped the soldiers during battle.

At least two women did take part in the battle at Monmouth Court House. One ran to her husband's side after he was hit by a British bullet. She fired back at the British. Another helped her husband work a cannon. During the battle, a British cannonball is said to have passed between her legs, tearing away much of her skirt. She kept working.[3]

Molly Pitcher was not a real person. Her legend represents several actual women who served the American cause bravely in battle.

This 1781 engraving depicts the American and French siege of the British army at Yorktown, Virginia. Washington's victory at Yorktown marked the last major battle of the American Revolution.

of 1776–1777 and 1777–1778. The battles of Trenton and Princeton gave the Americans hope. At Valley Forge, Washington's ragtag army became a more confident, effective fighting force. There were times during both winters when the Continental Army teetered on the brink of collapse. But the resolve of the soldiers and their officers kept the dream of independence alive.

TIMELINE

1775

On April 19, American colonists fight British soldiers at Lexington and Concord, Massachusetts. Under constant gunfire, the British retreat to Boston. The battles mark the beginning of the American Revolution.

On June 17, the British take Breed's Hill and Bunker Hill, outside of Boston. But they suffer heavy casualties in the battle.

In early July, George Washington takes command of the Continental Army.

1776

On March 17, the British army abandons Boston.

On July 4, the Continental Congress adopts the Declaration of Independence, which lays out the reasons for America's break with England.

On August 27, the British defeat American troops at the Battle of Long Island. Washington's army appears trapped on Brooklyn Heights. However, during the night of August 29–30, the Americans manage to escape across the East River to Manhattan.

More than 2,800 American troops are killed, wounded, or captured when the British take Fort Washington on November 16.

On November 21, Washington's army begins its retreat across New Jersey.

Washington's troops retreat across the Delaware River to Pennsylvania on December 7.

On December 25, Washington begins to move his troops back across the Delaware River in order to attack the British outpost at Trenton. The following morning, the Continental Army wins the Battle of Trenton, capturing about 900 prisoners. The army quickly retreats back across the Delaware River.

On December 30, Washington gathers his troops in New Jersey again for another attack.

1777

On January 2, Washington's troops clash with redcoats under the command of Lord Charles Cornwallis at and around Trenton.

Cornwallis believes he has Washington cornered along the banks of Assunpink Creek. However, Washington's troops slip away and march to Princeton, where they win the Battle of Princeton on January 3.

The British army, under the command of General William Howe, defeats Washington's army at the Battle of Brandywine on September 11.

On September 26, the British army enters Philadelphia. Congress has fled to York, Pennsylvania.

At the Battle of Germantown, on October 4, the Continental Army surprises British troops but is forced to retreat.

In December, Washington's army straggles into Valley Forge to set up its winter camp.

1778

In March, Nathanael Greene becomes quartermaster general. Also that month, the Prussian volunteer Friedrich Wilhelm von Steuben begins teaching the Continental Army how to drill and become more disciplined.

Continental troops celebrate the signing of an alliance with France on May 6.

On June 28, British and American troops battle to a draw at Monmouth Court House in New Jersey.

1779–1783

Most of the fighting shifts to the south. In 1780, the British win major victories in Charleston, South Carolina (May), and Camden, South Carolina (August).

The Americans under General Nathanael Greene cripple a British force under General Charles Cornwallis at Guilford Courthouse in North Carolina on March 15, 1781.

Lord Cornwallis surrenders his army at Yorktown, Virginia, on October 19, 1781. This is the last major battle of the American Revolution.

On September 3, 1783, the Treaty of Paris is signed. It officially ends the war. The British recognize American independence.

CHAPTER NOTES

CHAPTER 1: DESPERATE TIMES

1. John Buchanan, *The Road to Valley Forge: How Washington Built the Army That Won the Revolution* (Hoboken, N.J.: John Wiley & Sons, 2004), pp. 68–72.
2. David Hackett Fischer, *Washington's Crossing* (New York: Oxford University Press, 2004), p. 114.
3. Gordon W. Wood, *The American Revolution: A History* (New York: Modern Library, 2003), p. 78.
4. Gary L. Gregg II and Matthew Spalding, *Patriot Sage: George Washington and the American Political Tradition* (Wilmington, Del.: ISI Books, 1999), p. 71.
5. Fischer, pp. 115–117.
6. Ibid., pp. 2–4.
7. Ibid., p. 134.
8. John Ferling, *A Leap in the Dark: The Struggle to Create the American Republic* (New York: Oxford University Press, 2003), p. 188.
9. Fischer, p. 190.
10. Bruce Chadwick, *The First American Army: The Untold Story of George Washington and the Men Behind America's First Fight for Freedom* (Naperville, Ill.: Sourcebooks, Inc., 2007), p. 137.

CHAPTER 2: ATTACK IN THE SNOW

1. John Buchanan, *The Road to Valley Forge: How Washington Built the Army That Won the Revolution* (Hoboken, N.J.: John Wiley & Sons, 2004), p. 161.
2. John Bradley, *Washington Crossing Historic Park: Pennsylvania Trail of History Guide* (Mechanicsburg, Pa.: Stackpole Books, 2004), p. 21.
3. Bruce Chadwick, *The First American Army: The Untold Story of George Washington and the Men Behind America's First Fight for Freedom* (Naperville, Ill.: Sourcebooks, Inc., 2007), p. 141.
4. David Hackett Fischer, *Washington's Crossing* (New York: Oxford University Press, 2004), p. 217.
5. David McCullough, *1776* (New York: Simon & Schuster, 2005), p. 276.
6. Ibid., p. 279.
7. Fischer, p. 230.
8. McCullough, p. 281.

9. Ibid., p. 282.
10. Chadwick, p. 149.
11. Fischer, p. 313.
12. Chadwick, p. 159.

CHAPTER 3: THE CAMP AT VALLEY FORGE

1. John H. Ansley, Jr., *Valley Forge: Triumph of Spirit* (Devon, Pa.: Lazy Dog Group, 2000), p. 6.
2. Thomas Fleming, *Washington's Secret War: The Hidden History of Valley Forge* (New York: Smithsonian Books/HarperCollins, 2005), p. 89.
3. Ibid., p. 12.
4. Ibid., p. 25.
5. John Buchanan, *The Road to Valley Forge: How Washington Built the Army That Won the Revolution* (Hoboken, N.J.: John Wiley & Sons, 2004), p. 294.
6. Wayne Bodle, *The Valley Forge Winter: Civilians and Soldiers in War* (University Park, Pa.: The Pennsylvania State University Press, 2002), p. 168.
7. Oscar Reiss, *Medicine and the American Revolution* (Jefferson, N.C.: McFarland & Co., 1998), p. 188.
8. Bodle, p. 168.

CHAPTER 4: FORMING A FIGHTING FORCE

1. Thomas Fleming, *Washington's Secret War: The Hidden History of Valley Forge* (New York: Smithsonian Books/HarperCollins, 2005), p. 218.
2. Wayne Bodle, *The Valley Forge Winter: Civilians and Soldiers in War* (University Park, Pa.: The Pennsylvania State University Press, 2002), p. 201.

CHAPTER 5: OUT INTO THE FIELD

1. John Ferling, *A Leap in the Dark: The Struggle to Create the American Republic* (New York: Oxford University Press, 2003), p. 216.
2. Thomas Fleming, *Washington's Secret War: The Hidden History of Valley Forge* (New York: Smithsonian Books/HarperCollins, 2005), p. 317.
3. Ibid., p. 321.

GLOSSARY

alliance—An agreement or treaty between two or more nations.

barrage—A heavy round of artillery fire designed to protect advancing or retreating troops or to stop enemy troops from advancing.

cabal—A small group of secret plotters, often against a government or a person in power.

casualties—Soldiers who are killed, wounded, or captured by the enemy.

enlistment—The period of time a person is signed up for military service.

Hessian—A German professional soldier hired by the British to fight against the Americans during the Revolutionary War.

incentive—Something offered, such as an award or bonus, to get someone to do something.

morale—The state of mind (for example, confident, excited, worried, or discouraged) of a person or group.

outpost—A military base located away from the main part of the army.

primary source—A document, text, or physical object which was written or created during the time under discussion.

quartermaster general—The person in charge of providing food, clothing, transportation, and shelter for an army.

quarters—Lodging; the place where a person or group sleeps.

rations—A soldier's daily supply of food.

rebellion—An uprising against authority or against the government.

redcoat—A British soldier during the Revolutionary War.

skirmish—A battle between small groups of soldiers rather than entire armies.

FURTHER READING

Books

Allen, Thomas B. *Remember Valley Forge: Patriots, Tories, and Redcoats Tell Their Stories.* Washington, D.C.: National Geographic, 2007.

Fleming, Thomas. *Everybody's Revolution: A New Look at the People Who Won America's Freedom.* New York: Scholastic Nonfiction, 2006.

Freedman, Russell. *Washington at Valley Forge.* New York: Holiday House, 2008.

Murphy, Jim. *The Crossing: How George Washington Saved the American Revolution.* New York: Scholastic Press, 2010.

Internet Addresses

National Park Service: Valley Forge National Historical Park
<http://www.nps.gov/vafo/index.htm>

Washington Crossing Historic Park
<http://www.ushistory.org/washingtoncrossing/>

INDEX